Stop Selling to Yourself!
Learn the "E-Har-Money" of selling
and
CLOSE MORE SALES!

Tom "The Bug Man" Bray

with

Cathi Bray

"He who knows others is wise;

he who knows himself is enlightened."
— Lao Tzu

Stop Selling to Yourself!
Learn the "E-Har-Money" of selling and
CLOSE MORE SALES!

Contents:

Introduction

If you are happy with your current closing rate, you can stop reading this book and give it to someone that needs it. But if you think a higher closing percentage sounds good, then keep reading and get ready for what I call, the "E-Har-Money of selling"! Let's face it, E-Harmony is as successful as it is because they do, what? They match you with someone you relate well with, someone you have things in common with. Well, let's do that with your sales calls! We can call it "C-Har-Money" – or "Closing Har-Money." But instead of only finding customers that are like you, I'll teach **YOU** how to relate to **ALL** potential customers. You will **BE** the ultimate match for everyone you come across! More closed sales mean more harmony with your boss, your spouse, and your bank account. I will help you relate better with all the temperaments and harmonize with them no matter what their personality.

Sales can be a very challenging career choice, but in reality, we are all in sales to one degree or another.

Selling is simply trying to relate to another person, and in the process, to gain something for yourself. We typically think of selling something for money; however, as in the dating world and life in general we are really just selling ourselves. Actors and radio talk show hosts sell you on their movie or TV show to get ratings, which generate more revenue. Most of the world revolves around getting others to like you, or to buy or support your product or service, so selling is a key element in our world today.

Learning to relate to others is big business, and big money. Look at all the dating services out there. Years ago, E-Harmony launched a new way to find a mate. By studying the personalities, likes, dislikes, and other aspects of their members through a database, they help people find someone special in a way that 30 or 40 years ago was considered crazy or only the work of desperate people. Now, there are many other sites just like that one, all helping lots of folks find happiness by matching their personalities to one another.

This book is based upon a similar concept, but applying it to a sales setting. We will teach you how to relate, very quickly, to all types of people and to become a better sales person, who not only meets the needs of your customers, but who is able to put more money in your pocket at the same time.

People who enter the sales field are trained by their company in a certain method of selling, which usually consists of gaining entry to the home of a potential customer, sitting down with them at the kitchen table and going over a beautiful presentation, page after page, all leading the customer to the point of purchase. The problem is that many sales people are trained to present, but not to close the deal. They really are not trained to quickly assess their customer and meet their needs, which is what must be done in order for everyone to feel like they have just participated in a great deal.

I have been involved in direct selling for many years, primarily in the pest control/termite industry, but also in various multilevel marketing businesses. I've worked for several of the top pest control companies in the nation, and have found that by applying these principles my closing percentage has soared above others who have been in the business much longer than I have.

Around ten years ago, I decided to stop working for others and I started my own company. In just a few short years, by applying what I'm teaching you here, we have built a successful company that brings in more than enough to support our family. You can do the same. All it takes is learning how to relate to other people, caring enough to meet their needs, and ending up with a win-win situation for all concerned.

It really is that simple. There are some concepts you need to learn, though, which you may not be familiar with yet; and that is where I come in. So, let's get started and learn how to sell!

Chapter 1

Stop Selling to Yourself!

> *"People generally sell to others the way they, themselves, like to be sold to."*

Let the above quote sink in for a minute and see if it applies to you. People generally sell to others the way they, themselves, like to be sold to. We know what works for us, and we are comfortable with that method, we believe it is the best method; but is it right for everyone?

Two people can take the same sales presentation and both will add something of their own that makes them feel comfortable, but it may not be right for the object of that presentation – the customer. After all, our subconscious mind controls much of what we have programmed it over the years to respond to, or to do things in a way that is familiar and comfortable to us. Some things, such as scents, trigger a certain response in us because of what is programmed into our subconscious mind. And even in sales, we tend to do this without thinking about the way we react. The way we present our product is because of what is programmed into us through our past experiences, and especially through our temperament, or personality.

As an example, if you sell something to me I want your pitch to be short, sweet, and to the point. I don't want to hear all the specs and what the product is made of, where the parts come from, etc. I just want you to give me the bottom line. I also want to haggle a bit on price, but not ad nauseam. Too much detail and too much time spent, and you will lose me. If you sell to Cathi, she is going to want to hear the details, and then have time to think about it and research it before she makes a decision.

So, when we go out to sell something, we might naturally sell that way to others – all others, not considering that people are different and need to be sold to differently. We all naturally revert back to what feels comfortable to us, especially when things get tough. Let's face it, when you work in sales you deal with a lot of rejection and may begin to take it personally. When we are hurt, we seek comfort. We may feel good about ourselves because we like what we hear coming from our own mouth, but it is not always what's right for the customer. That's what I call "selling to yourself."

Selling to yourself is easy to do, because it fills a need in us; it is programmed into us through our temperament and our life. That is why the E-Harmony-type programs work so well. Those systems take who you are and match it with others who share similar traits. However, in sales, you are not looking for one mate; you are looking for multiple connections each day, leading to more sales each day, and to more money! After all, success breeds success, and the more you are able to sell to the other temperaments, the more money you will make. This will lead to more confidence, and the confidence will make you more sales. More sales make more money, which can lead to promotions and better quality of life. So, the bottom line is that good things happen when you make more money!

"What if the acceptable closing percentage could be raised?"

People, and companies, sometimes settle for much less than they deserve and can achieve. What if the acceptable closing percentage could be raised? Remember that people used to think your heart would explode if you ran the mile in less than four minutes? Of course, once that was accomplished by Roger Bannister, everyone began doing it. That's what we need to do with our concept of closing percentages – stop thinking of 25-30% as acceptable and reach for 75% - 100%!

When I was being trained at one of the top pest control companies in the nation, I was told that they needed me to close 25-30% of my leads to remain effective to them. I had never had a job in sales before, so my first thought was, "Why so low?" That was the average closed by the company's top sales people, so that was the standard they set for others. (And being naïve, I didn't know at that time how hard it was to even sell that much sometimes.) We were not given any new information or techniques at that job, though, just expected to contact more people, since, after all, "selling is just a numbers game."

Prior to working for that company, I had learned about the four basic personality profiles, or "temperaments," and I saw that this concept could translate well to my position in sales. The system I was taught at the time was "Personality Plus," by Florence Littauer. Personality profiling has been taught by others with various approaches – some use colors to designate the personalities, some use animals – but the basics remain the same.

So, let's learn about the temperaments and see if this system will help you, not only in your sales position, but in your life, in general.

The concept of four basic temperaments is a proto-psychological (early psychological) theory that suggests there are four basic, fundamental personality types. In the original system put forth by Hippocrates, who used it in his medical practice, the types were labeled: Choleric (**kol**-er-ic), Sanguine (**sang**-gwin), Melancholy (**mel**-*uh* n-kol-ee), and Phlegmatic (fleg-**mat**-ik).

You may find some systems that use color labels: red, yellow, blue, green; and some use animal labels: otter, golden retriever, beaver, and lion – and there are others – but those don't matter, because as a true Choleric, we're doing it MY way! The Melancholies are free to research all others and then agree with me; the Sanguines are free not to care, but to discuss it, and several other topics, with everyone they meet; and the Phlegmatics just need to agree and enjoy the ride.

Obviously, I'm kidding; but all kidding aside, we will take a closer look at each of the four types in later chapters and see if you find yourself in them, as well as your business partners, friends, or family members. After that, you'll learn how to apply the temperaments to your sales position and improve your bottom line dramatically.

To give you a quick, bottom-line breakdown: Cholerics are the highly ambitious types that are born leaders. They take charge and are strong and assertive. Sanguines are the pleasure seekers. They are very sociable, the happy types that never meet a stranger. Melancholies are the highly analytical types, very detail oriented, organized, and literal. And Phlegmatics are the relaxed, thoughtful, laidback peacemakers.

If, as I believe, we naturally sell the way we like to be sold to, and if there are four basic temperaments/personalities, which there are, that means you will have a customer who likes your approach approximately 25% of the time. That's one out of the four personality types. So, you will relate well to 25% of your customers. Funny, that's the same closing rate the company I worked for wanted – at least 25%! And you will naturally close a few more sales from people who like the company you represent, or who are just ready to buy from the first person they find; and that will bring your numbers up a few percentage points.

But let's think this over: If you are the same temperament as 25% of your customer base, you feel great with those customers, but you may struggle to relate to the other 75%. What if there was a way for you to relate better to that group, the other 75%? Would you close more sales and make more money? Hell, yes! Selling to yourself feels natural and good for your ego, because it is easy, but it leaves money on the table and out of your pocket.

Most companies teach you a technique based upon their leadership, or manager's, style. They likely teach a sales presentation technique, but do not focus on the individualism of the customer. Teaching how to relate to your customer should be the top priority in training new sales staff. By relating to each person, and selling to them the way **THEY** like to be sold to, your closing rate will go through the roof! You will also build loyal customers, who will promote you to others, which is what you want – word-of-mouth marketing from loyal customers!

As I mentioned in the Introduction, if you are happy with your current closing rate, you can stop reading this book and give it to someone that needs it. But if you think a higher closing percentage sounds good, then keep reading and get ready for what I call, the "E-Har-Money of selling"! Let's face it, E-Harmony is as successful as it is because they do, what? They match you with someone you relate well with, someone you have things in common with. Well, let's do that with your sales calls! We can call it "C-Har-Money" – or "Closing Har-Money." But instead of only finding customers that are like you, I'll teach **YOU** how to relate to **ALL** potential customers. You will **BE** the ultimate match for everyone you come across! More closed sales mean more harmony with your boss, your spouse, and your bank account. I will help you relate better with all the temperaments and harmonize with them no matter what their personality.

To expand on our previous description of the temperaments, I'll give you a bit more insight now, and we will go into depth on the strengths and weaknesses of each temperament in later chapters. We will also discuss how each sales person's temperament guides the way they approach sales, and we will get into more specific examples of how to approach each customer, based on their temperament.

If you are a Choleric, you are ambitious and a born leader. You can be very assertive and have a lot of energy and passion; and you will likely try to instill that in others. You are very task oriented and are greatly focused on getting the job done efficiently. You are part of the do-it-now group, and you tend to dominate others with your strong will and opinions. You can even become dictatorial and tyrannical if you are not careful. You like to be in charge and are likely to be an excellent planner in the sense of seeing the big picture and knowing where you, or your organization, should go; but not in the sense, necessarily, of planning the details of how to get there. You easily find solutions to problems and enjoy the process.

As a Sanguine, you will be fundamentally sociable and pleasure-seeking, and could be impulsive and charismatic. You enjoy social gatherings, making new friends, and can be the life of the party. You are usually quite creative in some way, and may be chronically late to appointments, because you get caught up in talking to people and enjoying the moment. You can lose interest in a new hobby or task when it ceases to be engaging or fun, but you are also a people-person and warm-hearted, lively, and optimistic.

If your primary temperament is Melancholy, you tend to be cautious as you study, research, and examine all aspects of a situation or task before taking it on. You can be a perfectionist with a high degree of personal excellence, which leads to self-reliance and independence. Melancholies tend to prefer to do things themselves, so that they can maintain their high standards. You are great with details and planning, and love charts and graphs, but this can also slow down your progress because you tend to want things to be perfect before you move forward.

As a Phlegmatic, you are everybody's pal. You are most likely relaxed and quiet, and probably very content and kind. Phlegmatics may range from warmly attentive to lazily sluggish, so keeping your energy level up will be very important to you. You are very consistent and dependable, and can be relied upon to be a steady and faithful friend. You are accepting, affectionate, and make friends easily, and would be a good diplomat, because you tend not to judge others and are a peacemaker. You prefer to observe and to think on the world around you sometimes, but not necessarily get involved. You may be shy and not fond of change and uncertainty. You are generally calm, rational, curious, observant, and considerate; but may become passive-aggressive if you do not learn to properly communicate your desires to others.

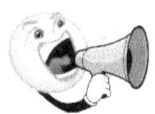  

Can you see yourself in those descriptions? How about your family members, friends, and coworkers/boss? As you look deeper into the temperaments, you will see that we all have a primary temperament and a secondary temperament. This does not complicate things in a short-term sales relationship, because the primary temperament is usually all you need to identify to relate well to your customer. When we talk about each temperament in more detail, we will discuss the variations of each, along with their secondary traits that can affect how the personality is rounded out.

> *"When it comes to being sold, I want it to be short and to the point..."*

So, to make it personal, I will show you how the temperaments affect my personality and how I make decisions. I am primarily a Choleric, with a Melancholy secondary. When it comes to being sold, I want it to be short and to the point, and I don't want my time wasted with too much information.

I will have done my own research before we meet, so that I can make sure you know your product or service well, and I will test you during the process.

Now, if I sell to others the way I like to be sold to, what would happen? I would do great with the other Cholerics, who like the same methods I do, and I could probably push a number of the easy-going Phlegmatics my way; but I would likely lose all the Melancholies, because I will leave out too many details; and I would definitely lose the Sanguines, because I didn't take the time to listen to their stories and make the interaction fun.

In that scenario, 25% of my potential customers are with me, the Cholerics, plus maybe 5% of the Phlegmatics that were not too intimidated by my aggressive personality, and possibly 3% of the others that were just ready to buy (although I realize I wouldn't get all 25% of the Cholerics, but just for demonstration purposes we'll go with those numbers). At that point, I am closing about 33% of my sales, which would put me top in sales at many companies. Now, if I can adapt and not sell to others the way I like to be sold to, but really put my customers first by considering their needs and desires, things change dramatically – and it's not as hard as you might think.

> ***"I am now closing 63% of my sales, and I'm a super star!"***

By learning to sell to the other temperaments, if I pick up just 10% of the other three personalities, I am now closing 63% of my sales, and I'm a super star! That means my income just jumped 30% - not a bad raise! How many sales managers would love an increase that big in their sales team? Let me give you a couple of examples of how I used this knowledge in one of my previous jobs, and how it gave me sales that I wouldn't otherwise have closed.

Because of my closing percentages at a previous company, I was asked to shadow a salesman that was, at that time, closing only about 15% of his leads. We were called out to a house for rodent issues. When we got to the house, we did the inspection and discussed the treatment options with Mrs. Homeowner, and sold her a $250 rodent treatment – she was ready to buy and get rid of those varmints!

During our inspection, however, we also found that the house had termites in three areas. This opened up a much larger sales opportunity, but Mrs. Homeowner was not prepared to make that decision and needed to discuss it with Mr. Homeowner. She asked us to come back when her husband was home. When we came back at the appointed time, we met with Mr. Homeowner and discussed the rodent plan, then went outside to look at the termite issues and came back in to discuss the treatment options.

So, let's determine Mr. Homeowner's temperament right now. When we discussed the rodent issues with him, all he wanted to know was how long it would take to get rid of them. He never seemed concerned with the details, so let's rule out the Melancholy personality. He was also not very chatty and did not smile, never asked my name or gave me his, so we can rule out Sanguine. That narrows him down to Choleric or Phlegmatic. From there, I just guessed, since my odds were 50/50. No, just kidding. Again, he never smiled and didn't need to know my name, he did not care about being friendly or nice, just wanted to get this handled and move on.

A Phlegmatic would have been much more easy-going and personable, so Choleric was the easy choice. (Sometimes you can even guess the temperament of the unknown spouse by knowing the temperament of the husband/wife, which may help you prepare to deal with them, because as we know, opposites usually attract.)

Now, the company we worked for at the time had a very nice brochure that walks the customer and the sales person through the termite treatment steps in very nice detail. This company trains and expects each sales person to cover the entire brochure, from front to back. It is an awesome sales tool that is well put-together and made by a very detailed Melancholy person, as you might now be able to understand. The process is to sit down at the kitchen table with the customer and go through the brochure, page by page.

I was there to observe the other sales person in action, remember? After we got back inside, Sales Guy asks Mr. Homeowner to join him at the table to discuss the treatment plan. This is when a couple of important factors came into play. First, Sales Guy headed to the formal dining room table that was a show piece and was probably only used once a year, instead of the kitchen table. Not a very comfortable and casual location. Secondly, I noticed our customer roll his eyes and drop his head to one side at that time. Mr. Homeowner and I were standing near the stairs in the foyer when I noticed his body posture change, and the fact that Sales Guy was heading to the formal dining room and Mr. Homeowner was not.

"...the customer sat down on the stairs and relaxed a bit."

There was a small stool near me in the foyer, so I sat down and began directing my comments toward the customer. Since we had already figured the price, I was ready to close the deal. As I began talking about the price while sitting on the stool, the customer sat down on the stairs and relaxed a bit. I explained the way we figured his price, by the lineal foot, gave him the bottom line of $900, and I shut up. He then looked up at me and asked if I would do it for $800. I got up, took a step, stuck out my hand, and said, "You have a deal." Our Sales Guy was sitting alone at the dining room table wondering what was going on out in the foyer.

What we had was a very extreme Choleric personality in our customer. Remember, we Cholerics don't want our time wasted by going through your pretty brochure, we want the bottom line and we want it done, and done right, at a fair price. When Melancholy Sales Guy made his patented move toward the dining room, he left Choleric Customer behind. I could tell we were losing him quickly, so I made my patented find-a-spot move, and Mr. Choleric joined me. He knew I was not going to sit on that little stool very long, so he plopped down on the stairs and we had ourselves an impromptu business meeting.

My presentation to him was simply to tell him how I arrived at my price, what the total was, and how the work would save his home. I knew he would want to bargain some, which most Cholerics do, so I was willing to give him what he wanted – a short, direct sales pitch, without a long, detailed presentation, and with just enough wiggle room in the price to allow for some negotiation.

Our Sales Guy in this example was a very Melancholy personality, who was selling to all of his customers the way he would like to be sold to. It felt natural and comfortable to him, but he lost more than he sold.

In another example, with a twist, I went out on a call alone and met Mrs. Sanguine. I was sent on this call for a routine termite inspection. At the time, the company was using Secret Shoppers to evaluate our sales people.

Secret Shoppers get paid to have sales people come into their home and give a presentation of what they offer. Obviously, the sales people do not know the customer is a Secret Shopper. SS's do this to make extra money and are given an evaluation sheet from the company that asks specific questions so they can evaluate the sales person.

As soon as the homeowner opened the door on this occasion, I knew I had a Sanguine on my hands. All I had to do was say, "Hi, my name is Tom..." and she took it from there. As soon as I introduced myself, she introduced me to each of her children and asked if I had kids, but never allowed me to answer as she explained how crazy her day had been so far, and it was only 1:00 pm. She was very nice, but very talkative, so I knew I had to make this a fun experience. After she caught her breath, I was able to speak, and that is when the fun started for all of us.

I began to make balloon animals for her three children — yes, balloon animals, one of the best ice breakers you could ever hope to have in your sales tool box. It is not hard to learn to make a few simple balloon animals (the hardest part for most people is learning to blow them up without a pump, but you can carry a small hand pump with you), and those things will open doors for you that you never thought possible. But getting back to Mrs. Sanguine, my balloon animals started the party.

I invited her to come along on the termite hunt with me at that point, which she and the three kids did, joyfully. After we completed the exterior inspection, we moved inside to inspect the interior and to follow company protocol by going through each page of their Melancholy brochure.

Here comes the twist: The company had a little contest going on at that time where the Secret Shopper would hide a certificate somewhere in his or her house, so that if you were inspecting each room as you had been taught, you would find the certificate and get a cash reward. I realized I had a Secret Shopper when we got inside and the attic stairs had already been pulled down for me. Guess what I found in the attic? You bet, my certificate! She was on my side at this point, and was helping me to be successful.

"...the pest elimination party bus could be at her house the next day..."

Now it got even better. As we went through the house, I found various pest issues. After we finished the kitchen, she asked me how soon we could start getting rid of the pests. I explained that the pest elimination party bus could be at her house the next day (my actual words). She thought that was great and was ready to sign the paperwork, so I did what any red-blooded sales person would/should do at that point, I stopped my hunt and closed the deal.

Never, ever, ever keep selling when they are ready to buy! There was no reason to continue the hunt, as we had already determined she had pests; and since she was ready to purchase a treatment plan to take care of it, continuing to search would have been a waste of time. So, I stopped my bug hunt, shut up, and got the papers signed.

The best part of this story is that I sold a Secret Shopper! Secret Shoppers are doing this to **MAKE** money, remember? Very few of them actually purchase the product or service. But my Sanguine friend did have a need for service, and since I changed my natural Choleric traits and made my inspection a fun bug hunt, I sold to her the way she wanted to be sold to and got the sale. That, along with my balloon animals, was just the ticket for that particular circumstance.

So, let's go through the temperaments and discover why I was able to rule out the other personalities. Although it is usually very easy to determine a Sanguine right away, because of their outgoing, fun, and talkative personality, we can also rule out the others, just in case we need more validation. There was no way this customer was Melancholy, because she moved from one subject to another without taking a breath, and without any concern for the details. She was way too chatty and seemed to have no concern for time, so we can rule out the Choleric, bottom-line temperament; and she was just the opposite of the quiet, peaceful, relaxed Phlegmatic person. If you think of Sanguines as the Energizer bunnies of the world, you'll have a good picture of this lady, so it was an easy call.

This story took another turn, however, when my outside-the-box, but 100%-effective sale almost got me fired. I was called into the office later that day and told that I only scored an 80% on my Secret Shopper evaluation, and that six other sales people had Secret Shoppers that week and all got 100%.

Please note that **NONE** of the other six had made a sale to their Secret Shopper. I lost points because I did not cover each page of the brochure with her and my hunt did not go into each room of the house. Remember that after we inspected the kitchen, she said she wanted to buy, so I stopped the excursion and got the papers signed. In doing that, I did not need to go into each and every room of the house – the problem had already been identified. The funny thing was, I got no points for actually selling the Secret Shopper!

I was told I would be written up, and that if I did it again, I would be fired! Now, at this point, I, being the Choleric that I am, asked a few questions to clarify things a bit in my mind: #1. Has anyone at the company **EVER** sold a Secret Shopper? Answer: No. My response to that was that I must have just made company history! Would that be going into my file, as well? #2: What is more important, looking good on a score sheet, or closing a sale and making myself **AND THE COMPANY** money? Answer: The score! I need to insert an eye-roll emoji here, because that's all I could do at that point.

This scenario is one of the reasons I'm writing this book. When we lose track of ways to improve ourselves, we only hurt ourselves. Be willing to look at a different way of doing what you are doing now. This company was willing to lose sales in order to have a great set of Secret Shopper scores to report at the next manager meeting.

And to be clear, I'm not saying the company's sales presentation should be thrown out the window and never used. Just simply change the amount of material you throw at the customer and present the information in a way that meets that customer's needs and way of being sold, if necessary. Sometimes that means giving them the whole enchilada, sometimes, just a thumbnail sketch; but don't penalize the sales person because they make the call to do what's best in various circumstances.

The company I worked for at the time had a great brochure that covered a lot of material, way too much material for some, but not for all. I could take that brochure and shorten it up for the Cholerics, and maybe even do it as we walked and talked, not necessarily sitting at the kitchen table.

For the Melancholies, I would cover all of the details, and maybe even more! The Sanguines would need a shorter presentation, just like the Cholerics, but with a lot of fun and talking added in. Sanguines will generally jump from one topic to another and it will be hard to go through the entire presentation, as is, so be sure to take note of what might have been skipped and come back to it if it is important. Again, meet the customer where they are and stop selling to yourself!

> *"One sign of a great sales person is the number of referrals he or she gets from existing customers."*

The two previous examples are just the tip of the iceberg, but they show how the sales could have been lost without selling to the customer the way they wanted to be sold to. The gentleman in the first example personally gave me three referrals of friends in his neighborhood, because he enjoyed the way he was treated. All three referrals led to termite treatments.

One sign of a great sales person is the number of referrals he or she gets from existing customers. Referrals come when you make the sales experience more than just a transaction, you relate to the customer on a personal level and make them feel comfortable. That customer actually told me he appreciated the way I respected his time and made it simple so he could move on to his next task, and that is why I got three more sales out of it.

Now, let's take a deeper look at each of the temperaments in order to fully understand each one...

Chapter 2
A Deeper Look

"So, what you see is not always what you get…"

As we learn the temperaments, we have to be careful not to put people into a box. We are all a complicated mix of our lives and experiences that can influence every part of us. Sometimes people are born with a natural temperament, say Choleric, but learn very early on that in order to function in their family, they have to put on a mask and act differently. Many times, a Choleric child born into a family with two Choleric parents – it happens – learns that they must put on a Phlegmatic mask in order to thrive. That is not a healthy situation, but one that happens in many families.

There might be a naturally Phlegmatic child that upon the death of one parent and the necessity for the other parent to work long hours in order to provide for the family, must act as though they are Choleric in order to manage the other children and the household in the parent's absence. Again, not ideal, but something you may run into.

So, what you see is not always what you get, but whatever dominant personality is being displayed by a customer at the time you are working with them, is the temperament that will be used to interact with you and to make decisions; so regardless of the person's natural tendencies, you can still be pretty confident in your approach if you meet the needs of the temperament you are presented with.

Another issue I touched on earlier is that we all have a primary temperament and a secondary temperament, and at times, those secondary traits may influence the person more than you think.

Basically, the two extroverted temperaments are the Choleric and the Sanguine; the two introverted being the Melancholy and the Phlegmatic. Let's look at the differences between the combinations of Choleric/Sanguine (C/S) and the Choleric/Melancholy

(C/M). (As a side note, you will rarely find someone displaying two completely opposite temperaments, such as Choleric/Phlegmatic or Sanguine/Melancholy, although through masking and life experience, anything is possible.)

A Choleric/Sanguine (C/S) is going to be a much more outgoing person than a Choleric/Melancholy (C/M); in fact, the C/S will be the most outgoing personality of them all! The C/S is going to be 200% "out there," the most extroverted of the temperament combinations. These will typically be your loud, boisterous, friendly people that may shake your hand completely off, drag you into their house, and shove a baby (or pet) into your arms, while jumping from one topic to another before they suddenly make a decision and are ready to move on.

A C/M will be much more interested in the details than a C/S, and these traits combine to form a customer that will want to know it **ALL** – no, will **INSIST** on knowing it all!

At the same time, if the percentage of influence is reversed – more Sanguine/less Choleric (S/C) or more Melancholy/less Choleric (M/C), you can see that you would have even more interest in details by the M/C than by even the C/M, and that the M/C personality would even be a bit less outgoing. The S/C will be even more interested in fun than the C/S, and only a bit less "out there" on the extrovert scale. So, you can see how even within the combinations, there are variations.

Let's look at the Melancholy/Phlegmatic (M/P) and the Sanguine/Phlegmatic (S/P). An M/P will be primarily concerned with details, but is also mainly an introvert, so he/she will be less likely to demand his/her own way – and even less likely the reverse, the P/M, who is the most introverted of all the temperaments.

The Sanguine/Phlegmatic is a bit more outgoing, but will not necessarily be the life of the party that the S/C will be. And a Phlegmatic/Sanguine is probably just happy to be alive, and is possibly the easiest of the personalities to be around.

Can you see yourself, and others, in these descriptions? Of course, no one is completely, 100% one temperament, and as I've said, there are cases where someone must "mask" a different temperament in order to get along in their family or company; but we generally have two dominating temperaments that mold our personalities.

For instance, a Melancholy/Phlegmatic will be much more of an introvert than a Melancholy/Choleric. The first will feel they know the right way to do a task, but may not assert their will over someone else. The second will know exactly the right way to do things, and **WILL** insist that it be done their way.

A Sanguine/Phlegmatic will be the happiest person on the planet, but may never get anything accomplished. A Sanguine/Choleric, however, if they are having fun at their task, may conquer the world.

So, your basic temperament, combined with your secondary temperament, will tell us a lot about you and will tell you a lot about why others do what they do. In a sales situation, we will not concern ourselves much with the secondary temperament, as that may not always be clear in a short-term setting. We will show you how to identify the primary temperaments that guide your customers and their decisions, and by learning this you will be able to meet their needs better while benefitting personally, as well.

Although all of us truly are a combination of primarily two types, by studying the basic four personalities in depth we can begin to get a better feel for ourselves and others, and understand better how the combinations play out in the people we meet.

Let's now look at the basic temperaments in detail, learning the strengths and weaknesses for each…

"My way or the highway!"

Cholerics

Strengths: goal-oriented, good at delegating, fast-acting, born leader, decisive, confident, motivating, instinctively right, takes charge, sees the big picture, and is practical.

Weaknesses: short-tempered, unsympathetic, bossy, impatient, proud, argumentative, tactless, workaholic, manipulative, stubborn, intolerant, domineering, and unaffectionate.

Motto: My way or the highway!

"Do it my way – it will be fun!"

Sanguines

Strengths: Sociable, cheerful, cute, popular, funny, convincing, animated, inspiring, encouraging.

Weaknesses: Undisciplined, scatterbrained, show-off, unorganized, unpredictable, forgetful, inconsistent, restless.

Motto: Do it my way – it will be fun!

"My way is the right way…"

Melancholies

Strengths: Considerate, self-sacrificing, loyal, thoughtful, detailed, orderly, faithful, respectful, dependable.

Weaknesses: Pessimistic, depressed, introverted, suspicious, critical, too sensitive, negative, insecure, unforgiving.

Motto: My way is the right way – and I have the research to prove it!

"Either way is fine with me."

Phlegmatics

Strengths: peaceful, satisfied, patient, friendly, diplomatic, consistent, tolerant, listener, content, inoffensive, adaptable.

Weaknesses: Fearful, indecisive, lacking goals, worrier, lazy, reluctant, timid, indifferent, unenthusiastic.

Motto: Either way is fine with me.

Have you determined your own temperament yet? Take the test in the next chapter to make sure, and to identify your secondary temperament, as well.

Most of us will come out with a high score in two of the personalities, and with the highest score in just one; but if you happen to come out pretty evenly-spaced across the board, there are a few possible reasons for this: You are Phlegmatic, are okay with all of the choices, and can't make a decision; you are masking your true temperament and trying to be all things to all people; or you have been through so much in life, and learned how best to deal with things, that you really are much more balanced than the others.

In this situation, it would be helpful to have two or three other people take the test for you, so you can see how others view you and maybe get a better gauge of your true, natural temperament.

Chapter 3

The Temperament Test

*"Personality profiling has been taught
by others with various approaches –
some use colors to designate the
personalities, some use animals –
but the basics remain the same."*

Instructions: In each of the following rows of four words **ACROSS** on the next page, place an **"X"** or checkmark in front of the **ONE** word that **MOST OFTEN** (or most closely) applies to you. Continue through all 28 lines; be sure you choose a word from each row, even if you feel that none of them apply to you, but do not choose more than one word in each row.

If you are not sure which word best applies, ask a spouse or friend to pick one for you, or think of what your answer would have been when you were a child. (We have given a full description of each of these terms on Page 100 to help you.) After you have completed the "Strengths" chart, go on to the "Weaknesses" chart on the next page and do the same.

When you have completed both charts, fill in your answers on the scoring sheet on the next page, and you will begin to see your temperament take shape!

Strengths

1. ___Adventurous	___Adaptable	___Animated	___Analytical
2. ___Submissive	___Self-sacrificing	___Sociable	___Strong-willed
3. ___Considerate	___Controlled	___Competitive	___Convincing
4. ___Satisfied	___Sensitive	___Self-reliant	___Spirited
5. ___Planner	___Patient	___Positive	___Promoter
6. ___Orderly	___Obliging	___Outspoken	___Optimistic
7. ___Friendly	___Faithful	___Funny	___Forceful
8. ___Daring	___Delightful	___Diplomatic	___Detailed
9. ___Cheerful	___Consistent	___Cultured	___Confident
10. ___Mediator	___Musical	___Mover	___Mixes easily
11. ___Thoughtful	___Tenacious	___Talker	___Tolerant
12. ___Listener	___Loyal	___Leader	___Lively
13. ___Contented	___Chief	___Chart-maker	___Cute
14. ___Perfectionist	___Pleasant	___Productive	___Popular

Now go on to the Weaknesses chart on the next page...

Choose the word that describes you best from the list of words **ACROSS**, just as you did on the Strengths chart on the prior page. If you do not understand a certain word or term, refer to the definitions on Page 100.

Weaknesses

1. ___Undisciplined	___Unsympathetic	___Unenthusiastic	___Unforgiving
2. ___Fussy	___Fearful	___Forgetful	___Frank
3. ___Impatient	___Insecure	___Indecisive	___Interrupts
4. ___Plain	___Pessimistic	___Proud	___Permissive
5. ___Naive	___Negative attitude	___Nervy	___Nonchalant
6. ___Worrier	___Withdrawn	___Workaholic	___Wants credit
7. ___Too sensitive	___Tactless	___Timid	___Talkative
8. ___Doubtful	___Disorganized	___Domineering	___Depressed
9. ___Inconsistent	___Introvert	___Intolerant	___Indifferent
10. ___Slow	___Stubborn	___Show-off	___Skeptical
11. ___Loner	___Lord over others	___Lazy	___Loud
12. ___Sluggish	___Suspicious	___Short-tempered	___Scatterbrained
13. ___Revengeful	___Restless	___Reluctant	___Rash
14. ___Compromising	___Critical	___Crafty	___Changeable

Now, it is time to discover your temperament! Transfer the X's from the first two charts onto the scoring chart on the next page (the same words are on all the charts), and then add up your totals.

For example, if you checked "Animated" on the "Strengths" chart, check it on the scoring chart on the next page. (Note: The words are in a different order on this scoring chart, they are now listed under the temperament they apply to, so that you can see which temperaments the majority of your X's fall into.)

Scoring Chart – Strengths

Popular Sanguine	Powerful Choleric	Perfect Melancholy	Peaceful Phlegmatic
1. ___Animated	___Adventurous	___Analytical	___Adaptable
2. ___Sociable	___Strong-willed	___Self-sacrificing	___Submissive
3. ___Convincing	___Competitive	___Considerate	___Controlled
4. ___Spirited	___Self-reliant	___Sensitive	___Satisfied
5. ___Promoter	___Positive	___Planner	___Patient
6. ___Optimistic	___Outspoken	___Orderly	___Obliging
7. ___Funny	___Forceful	___Faithful	___Friendly
8. ___Delightful	___Daring	___Detailed	___Diplomatic
9. ___Cheerful	___Confident	___Cultured	___Consistent
10.___Mixes easily	___Mover	___Musical	___Mediator
11.___Talker	___Tenacious	___Thoughtful	___Tolerant
12.___Lively	___Leader	___Loyal	___Listener
13.___Cute	___Chief	___Chart-maker	___Contented
14.___Popular	___Productive	___Perfectionist	___Pleasant

Totals – Strengths

(Total each column and write the number of X's below)

_____   _____   _____   _____

Scoring Chart – Weaknesses

Sociable Sanguine	Competitive Choleric	Methodical Melancholy	Peaceful Phlegmatic
1. ___Undisciplined	___Unsympathetic	___Unforgiving	___Unenthusiastic
2. ___Forgetful	___Frank	___Fussy	___Fearful
3. ___Interrupts	___Impatient	___Insecure	___Indecisive
4. ___Permissive	___Proud	___Pessimistic	___Plain
5. ___Naive	___Nervy	___Negative attitude	___Nonchalant
6. ___Wants credit	___Workaholic	___Withdrawn	___Worrier
7. ___Talkative	___Tactless	___Too sensitive	___Timid
8. ___Disorganized	___Domineering	___Depressed	___Doubtful
9. ___Inconsistent	___Intolerant	___Introvert	___Indifferent
10.___Show-off	___Stubborn	___Skeptical	___Slow
11.___Loud	___Lord over others	___Loner	___Lazy
12.___Scatterbrained	___Short-tempered	___Suspicious	___Sluggish
13.___Restless	___Rash	___Revengeful	___Reluctant
14.___Changeable	___Crafty	___Critical	___Compromising

Totals – Weaknesses

(Total each column and write the number of X's for each below)

_____   _____   _____   _____

Combined Totals

(Now, add up your totals - Strengths + Weaknesses and put them below)

Sanguine   **Choleric**   **Melancholy**   **Phlegmatic**

_____   _____   _____   _____

Is your temperament clear? Do you see a definite primary and secondary type? Are you evenly spaced, with very little variation between the temperaments? Do you have none, or very little, in any one category? We will discuss all of these in future chapters, so let's keep going!

Chapter 4
You, the Sales Person

"…it is sometimes easier to identify the personality traits of others, rather than ourselves."

By now, you should have a pretty good grasp of not only your temperament, but that of many friends and family members, as well. In fact, it is sometimes easier to identify the personality traits of others, rather than ourselves. But if you were brutally honest in taking the test and/or had someone who knows you well take it for you, you should come out with a good, clear picture – and again, not to put yourself or anyone else in a box, but in order to meet the needs of others better.

Now that you have a better understanding of who you are, has it helped you see why you do things the way you do? Knowing your strengths and weaknesses is an excellent way to "know thyself," which in turn, will help you deal with the strengths and weaknesses in others. You will be able to relate to your spouse, your children, your parents, friends, and your customers much better now that you know why they do what they do, and how to work with their temperaments to meet their needs.

But we are here to learn how to apply knowledge of the temperaments to your career in sales. So, in every sales encounter you need to identify the customer's temperament as quickly as possible. Sanguines can be the easiest to identify. With my Secret Shopper friend, all I had to do was say, "Hello." By introducing yourself and asking how their day has been, you can learn a lot.

The Sanguines are waiting to tell you anything and everything. The Cholerics will be short and to the point: "Great. What-cha-got?" The Phlegmatics will be much more personable than the Cholerics, but not as chatty as the Sanguines: "I'm doing well. Thank you for asking. How are you doing today?" The Melancholies can be direct, like the Cholerics, but will be more open to telling you about a particular issue that could be on their mind, and may not have anything to do with why you are there; but since you asked how their day was going, they will tell you, and may add more details than you bargained for: "Not too bad. Sure do hate this weather, though. I always know when the rain is coming in – joints lock up so bad I can hardly walk." Melancholies will almost always include emotion in their answer – feelings are important to them.

And this point may hurt a bit, but if you fail to make a sale because you do not know your customer, it is your own fault, no one else's; but now you will have the tools to do that. I have heard these comments from sales people after failing to close a deal:

"The lady would not be quiet and listen to me." Talking about a Sanguine customer who wanted a new friend or experience.

"That guy was so rude! He was in a big hurry and I will have to call on him again," about a Choleric customer who wanted the short and sweet bottom line.

"She asked me more questions than I had answers for! She made me feel like I didn't know what I was talking about. She had definitely done her homework!" about a Melancholy customer who came to the meeting prepared.

"She wanted to wait and talk to a couple of friends before she made a decision," obviously relating to a Phlegmatic customer who had a hard time making decisions and needed to find someone to make it for her, or to validate her decision. By the way, she was looking for trust in the sales person so that she would feel confident making the decision herself, but failed to find that trust and needed to turn to others she knew she could depend on.

Be honest with me, have you ever said something along those lines? Have you ever blamed the customer for the way they reacted when they rejected you and said, "no," or simply, "not right now"? As I said earlier, we tend to stay in our comfort zone and will sell to people the way we feel comfortable; and we then take the easy road out by blaming it on the customer when the plan does not fall into place and we don't make the sale. But you will not be doing that again! Now you have a better way, and by learning this method, and practicing it, you will become a much more productive and profitable sales person!

Let's look at each type of sales person and see how each of their temperaments might relate to the customers and do a better job of selling to each of the other personality types…

Chapter 5

The Methodical Melancholy Sales Person

"Melancholies are really good at being creative and at problem solving."

If your temperament is primarily Melancholy, you probably think your way is the best, and you surely even have the research to prove it; but remember, numbers do not lie. Unless you close 100% of your sales, you can improve your closing percentage. So, let's delve deeper into your psyche and figure out how you work best and how best to relate to your customers.

As a Melancholy, you are more serious than some of the other temperaments and can be very persistent and schedule-oriented. You will usually be the most neat and tidy of all the temperaments, having a place for everything and everything in its place – or at least you will know where everything is among the chaos, if you are the more absent-minded professor type that is extremely intellectual but who can't remember petty details, such as what day it is.

You know there is a best way to do everything, and you intend to find out what that is. You are good at organizing and prioritizing, and you need to apply that to your schedule; otherwise, you will spend all of your time researching and never get out the door and sell – "analysis paralysis."

Melancholies are really good at being creative and at problem solving. They tend to be readers, and with all the research they do (just for fun), it is likely they have come across something similar in their studies and will apply that to the problem at hand. They may also be the inventors and can make life easier for others by coming up with new ways to solve a problem.

Consider the following examples of real-life situations I've experienced with Melancholy friends:

One of my friends, that I'll call "Ed," wanted to buy a new car. He researched them and decided on the Honda as the best car for his money. This Honda had a fuel efficiency display that showed him when he was driving at the best speed for optimal fuel economy. Well, Ed took that light to heart and would not, could not, drive outside that range, regardless of the speed limit on the road or whether driving faster would actually get him to his destination on time or not. He would arrive late almost every time we met – but he would call to tell me he would be nine minutes late, or twelve minutes late...based upon the best fuel economy, the prevailing trade winds, the alignment of the planets, factoring in the gravitational pull of the sun and moon...you get the idea. And I'm just kidding, of course, but only barely. He really did do that, and he really did call to tell me exactly when he would be there, based on his GPS.

Ed would leave late to begin with most of the time, not because he was not conscious of the schedule, but because everything would have to be packed into his vehicle perfectly before he left, including anything and everything he might need – you know, in case the apocalypse occurred when he was away from home – and inevitably, something would need more tweaking, or a better way needed to be found to make it all work exactly right. And yes, Ed is an extreme example of a Melancholy off the charts, but learning about Ed will make Melancholy traits very easy to spot.

And who but a Melancholy could invent things like those cool pantry organizers, where you can put the newer cans in the top and they will roll down so that the oldest ones are used first – like the soup racks in the grocery store? And what about the desk organizers, day planners, file folder hangers, label makers, sticky notes, highlighters, and millions of other products designed to solve problems and make the world more organized for all of us? Notice all the things around you that are designed to make life easier for everyone. Chances are, a Melancholy figured out how to do it.

"These are definitely the idea people who not only dream up the concepts, but who know how to follow through with the details to bring it to completion."

What about the shoe tree, for goodness sakes? And there are entire stores and industries designed for the sole purpose of helping us organize things. There is even a container store! And what about those people that will come to your home and design the perfect closet system for you? Only a Melancholy could pull that off. It's almost like having a life coach, but they would be closet coaches!

These are definitely the idea people who not only dream up the concepts, but who know how to follow through with the details to bring it to completion. And because of their ability to feel emotions deeply, many of our musicians, poets, writers, actors, and artists are also Melancholy.

So, to have a little fun - you might be a Melancholy if:

- You set an alarm on your phone to tell you it is time to **GET READY** for bed (yes, Ed did this);

- You iron your socks and underwear – or have that done at the cleaners;

- You label your label maker;

- You understand binary code, and like it;

- You own, or have owned, a calculator watch;

- You have plastic covering your car's floor mats, just as extra, added protection.

If you saw the movie, "Money Ball," with Brad Pitt, that is a great depiction of how a Melancholy personality can change the world with his/her understanding of the details in life. The movie is about the Oakland A's baseball team and how the main character (a Melancholy guy) figured out a way to draft players and build a team based upon nothing more than the numbers and the results the player produced in a given situation.

They prove the system works by breaking a record for the most consecutive wins, and without spoiling the movie for those that haven't seen it, the system works. This team took no-name players and built a winning team without a huge payroll, by using numbers to forecast the way baseball teams were built, and it was figured out by a Melancholy who saw a better way of doing things.

So, as a Melancholy sales person, mastery is in the details; it is the foundation of all you do; but you will have to understand that none of the other three temperaments will care as much about the details as you do. If you determine you have a Melancholy customer, congratulations! Enjoy discussing the finer points of the situation with him/her, but don't let yourself get so lost in the moment that you forget you have other appointments that day. Cut it off at some point, close the sale, and move on to your next conquest.

If your next customer is Sanguine, you can pretty much throw your details out the window. The Sanguine temperament is your complete opposite, and the very details you hold so dear do not mean anything to them; in fact, they may butcher the facts so badly when repeating them that it will be hard for you (who knows the truth) to keep quiet and not continually correct them.

You will have to force yourself to set aside all of your facts, figures, graphs, and charts, and just decide that you are going to enjoy the experience with the Sanguine, interject as many facts as you can during the exchange, and work to make your time with them enjoyable. By doing so, you will make a friend, and have a better chance of closing the sale. This is when you can bring out your balloon animal skills that I spoke of earlier.

> **"It really isn't personal;
> they just simply really do not care."**

Try not to take it personally that they are not interested in all of your research. It really isn't personal; they just simply really do not care. If you can set aside your needs and desires, and focus on theirs, going with the flow and following their lead, you can accomplish what you both desire – a solution to their problem, and a sale for you!

If Mr./Mrs. Choleric meet you at the door, expect that the visit will be short and sweet. Again, as with the Sanguine, they may not be very interested in all of your research, but they will want to hear some. If you can match your behavior to that of your customer, modeling them, so to speak, they will relate to you better and trust you more. So, when dealing with a Choleric, give them a few facts and then stop talking and let them take the lead. They will either ask more questions, which you will have the answers to, or they will give you their decision.

If their decision is negative, you might ask if they based their decision on something you can give them more information on, or that you can clear up for them, but don't push them past their limit. If they do not seem receptive, it might just be that they have other things on their mind. In that case, ask if you can email more information for them to consider when they have more time and get back with them at a later date. They will appreciate it and likely be more receptive the next time you meet.

When dealing with a Phlegmatic customer, they may be kind enough to sit and listen to your entire sales pitch, but don't expect them to make a decision without speaking to someone else first – **UNLESS** you have built a relationship with them and they trust you enough to have faith in what you are selling.

Phlegmatics are notorious for being indecisive, and this is not always because they don't trust themselves enough to make the right decision; sometimes it is just because they truly do not care either way. These are **NOT** the folks who have strong feelings one way or the other. The best way to help a Phlegmatic make a decision is to give them the information, but to be personable, not so analytical that they lose the personal relationship. If they get to know you, even in a short amount of time, and feel that you can relate to them and them to you, and they trust that you have their best interest at heart, they will be much more likely to go ahead and close the deal. If not, ask them who they trust to help them make the decision, and then suggest that you come back when that person can be there with them. It might be worth the return visit for you. Of course, then you will have to determine the temperament of their confidante and present to them, as well; but if you are determined to meet the needs of Mr./Mrs. Phlegmatic, you will do what it takes to make that happen.

"...she learned how to gently approach people in a very personable way that would win their trust..."

My wife, who is writing this book with me, and who has learned to do all of this so well that it's hard to pin a definite temperament on her, but who is definitely **NOT** primarily a Phlegmatic, does this really well in her writing career. She was a reporter years ago for a daily newspaper and would often need to get an interview with people dealing with very difficult circumstances.

She was the best at getting the interview when others couldn't, because she learned how to gently approach people in a very personable way that would win their trust, and to identify and appeal to their basic temperament. There were times that someone would not give an interview to anyone, or allow someone into a crime scene, but she was able to get in, because she learned how to relate and become trusted very quickly and to model herself and her approach to the temperament of those she was seeking to gain the trust of, regardless of her own natural temperament.

Your greatest challenges as a Melancholy will be:

- Not overloading other personalities with your facts and figures;

- Not taking someone's lack of interest personally;

- Lightening up a bit;

- Forcing yourself to get away from the computer and get out into the field;

Conquer these things, and you will soar to the top of the sales ladder!

Chapter 6
The Competitive Choleric Sales Person

"Your way of helping people is generally to challenge them…"

You, dear Choleric, are most likely the mover and shaker of your sales team – the alpha dog, so to speak. You may already have the highest closing rate of your peers, because you are the most extroverted of all temperaments and thus are willing to get out into the world and tell folks what they need to do. You may also be tops in your field because you thrive in a competitive environment.

However, as I said before, unless you are closing 100% of your leads, you can always improve, right?

As a Choleric, you have a quick, sharp mind, so it is easy for you to scan over, or briefly hear about the pros and cons of your product/service and to grasp it quickly. It would serve you well, though, to spend a bit more time learning more of the details, since you are going to be facing Melancholy customers about 25% of the time and you do not want to lose those sales. You may be great at quickly assessing the situation and making a snap decision that is absolutely right, but your customer may not be able to do that. Having more facts and figures in your arsenal will better equip you to meet the needs of those who require that information in order to make their decision.

Your way of helping people is generally to challenge them, a technique that may come across as being too tough or not accepting them the way they are – I'm just telling you how others may perceive you, and it's the truth. You are never satisfied with being average and are always seeking excellence – traits that can make you a workaholic, if you are not careful.

Cholerics are always blunt and to the point. To give you a personal example, my wife went to the store one morning and bought cookies to use in a recipe later that day. She needed to go back to the store for more ingredients later, leaving our twin, teenage sons at home while she was gone. She wrote a note that she placed on top of the cookies, which read: "Boys, gone to the store. Be back soon. Eat the cookies and I'll break your legs. Love, Mom." That's a Choleric note if I ever heard one. Needless to say, the cookies were still intact when she got back.

A Choleric will always rise to the occasion and take care of business, and don't **EVER** tell them they can't do something – unless you want them to focus all their efforts on proving you wrong. To give an example of a take-charge Choleric from Florence Littauer's "Personality Plus" book, Florence recounts the story of her daughter, Marita, who was flying from Canada to Spokane, Washington, then transferring on to Seattle.

When the flight landed in Spokane, the passengers were told the flight to Seattle had been cancelled, but they were given no explanation or instructions. Marita found a nearby gate with flight personnel and was able to get more information from them. She went back to her gate and posted herself on the podium there, giving information to all that requested it.

As Florence stated in her book, "As it became apparent the flight was going to be hours late, and there was mutiny brewing in her flock [the other passengers], Marita went to the Hertz counter and checked on the cost of renting cars to drive to Seattle. With all the facts in hand, she went back to her perch above the crowd and called for their attention. Everyone listened as she explained Plan B to them. She asked those who wanted to let Hertz put them in the driver's seat to raise their hands. She then divided them into groups of six, appointed a captain for each group to drive, and a treasurer to collect the money. As she led them off happily to Hertz, one woman said, "It's so nice of the airlines to hire a lovely girl to take care of us."

Obviously, Marita did not work for the airlines, but she took charge and took control so quickly, and so well, I might add, that everyone assumed she did. Marita's secondary temperament is Sanguine, so she was the perfect candidate to stand up, take charge, and get everyone where they needed to go.

So, you might be a Choleric if:

- You can whistle, or yell, and your children come running;

- You can say in two words what it takes others paragraphs to communicate;

- You get the idea two sentences into a conversation (if that long), and head off to solve the problem – leaving the other person wondering where you went;

- You believe in "tough love";

- You physically move people from one place to another;

- You are always being chosen by others to be in charge;

- You finally agree to take a vacation, but must see and do everything you can while you are there (because you know it will be years before you do this again), so your family comes home more exhausted than before they left. (This is also why the wives of many Choleric men choose to go on "girlfriend retreats" aka vacations where they can actually relax and not have "the General" running them ragged.)

In your role as a sales person, you will have no problems with other Cholerics, unless you do not allow the other Choleric to feel in control of the situation. It will be a short and sweet meeting, and you will likely walk away with the sale. If you are dealing with a Melancholy, however, you are going to have to pull those facts and figures out of your arsenal that we talked about earlier. Refuse to give Mr./Mrs. Melancholy the facts that they need, and they will think you don't know what you're talking about. They will not trust you and will think you are just blowing smoke.

You also need to give the Melancholies time to process the information you give them, and this is the temperament that you might end up making a second visit for. They may need time to check on what you have told them, to do their own research and confirm or deny what you have said, and dwell on it a bit before they are ready to sign on the dotted line. Allow them that time, and you will likely get the sale; push them, and they will put up a wall that you will not get beyond.

> ***"…you must learn to turn off the burners…and put your engine on idle for a while."***

If Mr./Mrs. Sanguine is your customer, **RELAX**, and enjoy your time with them. This will be **VERY** difficult for you to do, but you must learn to turn off the burners (or at least turn them down) and put your engine on idle for a while. Push a Sanguine and they will just think you are rude and disrespectful. They really will not care about the facts and figures, but you must take time to listen to their stories and relate with them (maybe contributing a story or two of your own), or you will lose them.

With a Phlegmatic customer, your greatest challenge will be not looking down on them. Phlegmatics are not as quick as you at making decisions, and as a Choleric, you may think of Phlegmatics as slow or unintelligent. They are most certainly not, but discussion of the product/service will not be nearly as important to them as the relationship and trust they seek to build with you.

You must learn to be patient with them, not rush them, and allow them to get to know you – even if it is only through a short conversation. Be real with them; be open with them; be honest with them; and show true concern for them. If you do those things, they will trust you and be in a much better position to make a decision in your favor.

Your greatest challenges as a Choleric are:

- Being able to relax and go with the flow;

- Being patient with others who need more time than you do to make a decision;

- Not looking down on people;

- Not intimidating people with your sometimes-overpowering personality – in other words, dialing it back a notch – or four;

- Not insisting that everything is done your way – in other words, be flexible.

Chapter 7
The Sociable Sanguine Sales Person

"As a Sanguine, everyone knows you as the life of the party."

You are the one that keeps everybody in the office in stitches with the telling and retelling of many hilarious stories; but if you don't stop the party at some point and get out of the office, you are not going to make any sales. It seems as though the Sanguine personality is the perfect sales man/woman, but if a Sanguine is not disciplined, they will be very busy and talk to a lot of people, but not actually end up bringing home the bacon. Everyone probably knows a sales person like this – they love their job, but they are as broke as a church mouse, because they never actually get around to selling.

You must learn to schedule your time and be disciplined if you intend to make it in sales. It could be a great career for you, with the variety and flexibility it offers, as long as you treat it like a job, rather than a full-time party. Invest in day planners, calendars, an assistant, whatever it takes to keep you on track and productive, and you will do well.

I remember one sales guy at a previous job, who came in the office one morning and told us how he went to a customer's house the previous day and found termites, then went to the neighbor's house, because he met the neighbor while doing the first inspection, then ended up meeting at least seven other people from that block and talked to all of them about why he was there. He had a great time and met a lot of awesome people, most of whom had termite issues, but did not get one sale from all his time there. He was so busy having a block party that he never closed the sale on any of the customers.

He always had a great story to tell of his escapades each morning, but had horrible sales numbers – hence the need for all those organizational aids.

Sanguines are able to make friends with everyone, and will talk to a stump, if that's all they have for an audience. They are very descriptive when they speak and are enthusiastic and creative. They are also encouraging and supportive of others, and they never meet a stranger. They are everyone's sunshine on a gloomy day, and rarely get severely depressed.

Some people may describe a Sanguine as a roller-coaster ride or even as "bipolar," since their downs may come as quickly as their ups – but the downs won't be nearly as low as a Melancholy's downs may be. A Sanguine's downs are never very deep, and you can bring them up again very quickly just by asking them to retell a funny story.

Sanguines are notoriously forgetful of many details, but they can remember the color of the shirt you had on when they met you ten years ago. They also have big, wonderful, exciting ideas and plans, but are weak on the follow-through, unless they have a strong Choleric temperament as a secondary.

"Sanguines are notoriously forgetful of many details…"

I have a family member that is a strong Sanguine, and after just a simple trip to the grocery store, she will have met at least a few new best friends, and will spend 30 minutes telling you about each person's family, where they were born, and about all the physical ailments of each; but she will not remember how much she just spent on her groceries, which she probably walked out of the store without because she forgot that she bought them.

When selling to another Sanguine, you'll have to be extremely focused and intent on finishing up and actually getting back home that night; otherwise, the stories (and party) may go on for days. And since you enjoy the process so much, but tend to be weak on follow-through, learn how to close the sale. That is one of your greatest needs, besides organization. Enjoy your time with your fellow Sanguine, but at some point, let them know you are having a great time with them, but you must get on to your next appointment; and then ask for the sale. Tell them if they are ready to purchase, you'll be happy to get your product or service on its way to them asap.

If faced with a Melancholy customer, you will have to dial back your enthusiasm quite a bit, because some Melancholies will become even more withdrawn in the face of such happiness – or they may view your joy as silliness and feel you are not taking your job seriously enough. You will also need to pull facts and figures out of your arsenal, just like your Choleric counterpart, so focus on learning the details of your product or service when you are able; it will come in handy when dealing with one or two of the other temperament types.

You will also need to slow things down a bit for the Melancholy customer, because they need time to process what you are telling them, and to think about it before making a decision. If you rush them, they will say no, simply because they haven't had time to think about it and make an informed decision. Melancholies do not like to be rushed into things.

With a Choleric customer, you will also need to dial back your enthusiasm, and give them the **BASIC** information they need. A Choleric will get bored with how your Aunt Mary fell down the stairs and broke her leg when she was trying to kill a wasp that had flown into her open window because she was trying to let her daughter's room air out because she left wet clothes in the corner after going to her best friend's pool party at her dad's new house. Also, because of their temperament, the Choleric customer may look down on you and, just as the Melancholy did, feel you are not serious enough and not worth their time.

A Phlegmatic customer will be a captive audience for you, as long as you choose to entertain them. Again, you must use restraint here and not allow yourself to waste an entire day just because they are willing to listen. They will most likely trust you, though, and like you enough to give you the sale if you ask for it.

"If you really listen to people, they will tell you what they want/need."

Learn to be observant of your customer. Watch for signs of boredom: rolling eyes, looking off at other things, or checking their watch. If you see those things, get back on track and jump to the bottom line. Also, as we've said, facts **DO** matter to at least two other temperament types, so know your facts and figures and resist exaggerating them or brushing over them. Don't tell someone that your product will solve their problem every single time and that it is 100% effective if it isn't. They will not believe you, will not trust you, and will not give you the sale.

Learn to take notes. If you really listen to people, they will tell you what they want/need. Write those things down, whether you get the sale or not. It will help you become more attentive to others. And if you use your mobile device or a tablet to take notes on, just tell the customer you are taking notes so you can serve them better. That will keep them from thinking you are just distracted and texting someone else while they are talking.

And if you don't know the answer to a question, for goodness sakes, don't just make something up! Admit that you don't know the answer, but let them know you will find out for them, and then find out – don't forget to get back with them. You can most likely talk around any topic on earth, but in your sales job, you must stick to the product/service you are selling, know the benefits of them, and be able to focus on communicating those benefits to others.

You might be a Sanguine if:

- You come out of the shopping mall and not only don't remember where your car is, you don't even remember what kind of car you drive – but you do remember that it is red – and you end up with an entourage of strangers joining in to help you find the car, and enjoying every minute of it;

- You plan to visit 200 customers this week (unrealistic expectation), but only get in front of two;

- You realize after you get to work that your shoes don't match;

- You have tons of grand, creative plans, but have difficulty following through with them;

- You remember what you wore on the first day of school, every year of your life, but walk around looking for your phone so you can leave the house, while talking to your spouse – on your phone.

A Sanguine's greatest challenges will be:

- Learning to become organized and disciplined, which will serve you well in all areas of life;

- Learning to dial back the party a bit and get the work done;

- Learning to follow through on some of those grand plans;

- Listening to others and focusing on their needs.

Chapter 8

The Peaceful Phlegmatic Sales Person

"Phlegmatics are the most easy-going, content, and laid-back of all the temperaments."

You couldn't convince me that there are as many Phlegmatics in the sales industry as there are Cholerics, Sanguines, and even Melancholies. Phlegmatics, typically, just do not have the desire to be in sales in the first place – it is usually much easier for the Phlegmatic to work for someone else in a non-sales position, with set hours and expectations – with "easier" being the key word. But that is not always the case, especially for the Phlegmatic/Sanguine.

This temperament combination, the Phlegmatic/Sanguine, is likely in the game just to have fun and spend time with people, not so much to become Sales Man or Woman of the year. A Phlegmatic/Melancholy, however, would typically just be too much of an introvert to have the desire to spend all day out in the world talking with other people, but you never know where you'll find yourself in life.

Phlegmatics are the most easy-going, content, and laid-back of all the temperaments. These are the loyal friends that you have had since elementary school. They are happy to hang out with some of the more outgoing temperaments to live life vicariously through them. And the other temperaments love having them around, because Phlegmatics think whatever you suggest is awesome, and they rarely challenge your ideas.

Phlegmatics do have a stubborn streak, though, and once they decide to be in opposition to something, there is no convincing them otherwise. They are slow to make a choice, but once they do, it is usually set in stone.

The story is told of a man who had been married over 40 years to his wife and one day decided he wanted a divorce. Their children were dumbfounded, because they had never known him to speak a cross word with his outgoing wife and went along with everything she said. There was no talking him out of it, though, because as he said, "It has taken me 40 years to decide to leave. My mind is made up!" And in fact, it was!

If you are a Phlegmatic in the sales profession, you **MUST** learn to make decisions and to help others come to a decision, as well. This will probably be difficult for you, because you generally, really do not care one way or the other and /or you don't always trust your judgment and would rather have other people make the decisions for you.

Just as with the Sanguine, you will need to focus on being organized and disciplined, scheduling your day, in order to be most productive. If you are a Phlegmatic/Melancholy, that shouldn't be too difficult for you, since you have natural tendencies toward organization. If you are a Phlegmatic/Sanguine, you will have to work extra hard on that task. You will also need to know your product/service inside and out, so that you will be absolutely convinced, deep in your soul, of its benefits to others. By doing that, you will not hesitate to share with your customers, and you will be better able to help them come to a decision, as well.

If you are dealing with a Phlegmatic customer, this will be very important, but you will most likely endear yourself to him or her so well, that they will trust you to help them make the necessary decisions.

When dealing with a Melancholy customer, you will have the facts and figures they need, and will have the confidence to know that what you are saying is true and correct.

Your most challenging customer will be the Choleric, because you may have a tendency to allow them to bowl you over with their overpowering personality. Don't let that happen. Model their behavior. If they are speaking loudly, raise your volume to match. If they are short and to the point, you can do that, as well; but don't be intimidated and let them cut you off before you have given an accurate description of your product/service. Stand your ground; stand up to them; and have confidence when dealing with this temperament. They will respect you more when they see you have the guts to meet them toe to toe.

"Learn to show enthusiasm..."

Your Sanguine customers may rope you into their tales and fun, and you can lose an entire day in their world if you are not careful. If a Sanguine opens the door, check your watch and make a mental note to be out of there within "X" amount of time – 15 minutes, 30 minutes, whatever amount of time you feel necessary to do the job. Again, match their energy, and don't worry about talking over them. Sanguines generally do not mind being interrupted – if they get off track, they tend to forget what they were talking about anyway, but will eventually come back to it.

Sanguines talk over people all the time, so you will not offend them if you do the same. Just keep trying to bring the conversation back to your reason for being there, and then close the sale and move on.

Learn to show enthusiasm, especially around Sanguines and Cholerics. Doing this is not dishonest, it is matching your personality, at that moment, to another person so that you can each relate to the other more deeply. Phlegmatics can often lack enthusiasm, because obviously, they really just do not care one way or the other. Even if you don't care which option is chosen in a given situation, force yourself to be enthusiastic, and if one of the other temperaments asks you to choose, make the choice! If it doesn't matter to you either way, then just pick one and know that whomever asked you to make the decision will be thrilled that you did!

Motivating yourself will also become one of your most monumental tasks. Phlegmatics tend to be very content, and therefore, often lack the drive to get out and change things. They don't typically like change anyway, so rising above your current situation and becoming a better sales person will take great effort on your part, but you can do it.

You have what it takes to become successful, you just first must realize you want more, and then be willing to step outside your current comfort zone to get it.

Procrastination is another area of concern for Phlegmatics. "Don't put off till tomorrow what you can do today," should become your motto. And for our peaceful Phlegmatics, if working in a sales environment is stressful and chaotic but you choose to remain there, make sure your home is the most peaceful, relaxing place on the planet. Do whatever it takes to decompress on the way home each day, listening to soothing music, taking a long, hot bath when you get home, spending 30 minutes alone in a good book, stopping on the way home for a Yoga session – anything to bring you back to center and get you relaxed enough to do it again tomorrow.

Another of Florence Littauer's temperament stories describes a Phlegmatic very well, as recounted by the Phlegmatic's Sanguine/Choleric wife: "My Peaceful Phlegmatic husband has a dry sense of humor that comes from not taking life too seriously. When I met you, I was calling his office…to tell him that I had left the dryer on, and ask if he was going up to his…office, could he stop by the house and turn it off. His answer was simply not to worry about it; if the house burns down, we'll get another one. Then he added a quick little phrase as he hung up, 'I'm sure you paid that fire insurance bill that came last week,' knowing full well that I would never be the one to pay an insurance bill, or even know if we had any insurance! His unexpected humor can pull me out of a serious mood."

So, you might be a Phlegmatic if:

- You answer "Where do you want to go eat?" with "Doesn't matter to me; whatever you want is fine," EVERY…SINGLE…TIME!

- People love to have you around because you are never contrary with anyone; you always go with the flow;

- People describe you as "cool, calm, and collected";

- You are very content, but often lack the drive to make necessary changes in your life;

- You are a great mediator and friend, never judgmental, and rarely critical;

- You may remain in a bad situation much longer than you should, because it is just too much work to change things.

Some of your greatest challenges will be:

- Learning to motivate yourself and stop procrastinating;

- Having an opinion when necessary;

- Gathering up the energy to go out and do what needs to be done;

- Standing up to the more extroverted temperaments and not allowing them to run over you.

Chapter 9

Becoming the Best You

So, there you have it! You've learned that people really are different! You now know why other people act and react as they do, and why you do, as well. I hope you can see how this knowledge will help you in your sales career, but also in life, in general.

> *"Focus on your strengths,*
> *but work on your weaknesses."*

Don't get stuck in your temperament and continue bad habits, or weaknesses, by saying, "Well, that's just who I am." We can all change and improve. Study that list of strengths and weaknesses for your primary and secondary temperament. Decide on a few weaknesses that you'd like to change and work on those. Focus on your strengths, but work on your weaknesses.

Over time, if you really sink into this concept and work on yourself while relating better to others, you will probably find that your numbers when taking the test become more balanced. You may become one of those people that has trouble pinning down a specific temperament for yourself. But that's good, if it's because you are learning and growing; not if you are just putting on masks and trying to be all things to all people.

So, read the book again. Take the test for yourself, your friends, your family members, and your boss. Practice observing people and figuring out what temperament they are (and contact us about doing a workshop/seminar for your company or group). Then go out and close more sales! You can do it! We believe in you!

Appendix I

Personality Test Word Definitions

Strengths

1. Adventurous: Not afraid to do new and dangerous or exciting things.
2. Adaptable: Able to change or be changed in order to or work better in some situation or for some purpose.
3. Animated: Full of life and energy.
4. Analytical: Skilled in using analysis, especially in thinking or reasoning.

5. Submissive: Willing to obey someone else.
6. Self-sacrificing: Denying things to oneself for the benefit of others.
7. Sociable: Enjoying being around other people in a social setting.
8. Strong willed: Determined to have your own way.

9. Considerate: Thinking about the rights and feelings of others.
10. Controlled: Not overly angry or emotional.
11. Competitive: Wanting to win, generally at all costs.
12. Convincing: Causing someone to believe that something is true or certain.

13. Satisfied: To be content; not seeking more.

14. Sensitive: Aware of and understanding the feelings of other people.

15. Self-reliant: Confident in your own abilities.

16. Spirited: Full of courage or energy; very lively or determined.

17. Planner: Loves to have things thought-out and planned beforehand.

18. Patient: Able to remain calm and not become annoyed when waiting for a long time or when dealing with problems or difficult people.

19. Positive: Thinking about the good qualities of something or someone.

20. Promoter: A person that causes something to happen, or to become known by their enthusiasm and support of it.

21. Orderly: Having a place for everything and everything in its place.

22. Obliging: Willing to help; helpful in a friendly way.

23. Outspoken: Saying what they think, often without regard for another's feelings.

24. Optimistic: Always looking on the positive side of things; the glass is half full.

25. Friendly: Kind and helpful; showing support and approval.

26. Faithful: Having or showing true and constant support or loyalty.

27. Funny: Making people laugh.

28. Forceful: Having a strong and confident quality, expressed in a way that influences people's thoughts and ideas.

29. Daring: Willing to do dangerous or difficult things.

30. Delightful: Highly pleasing; a pleasant personality.

31. Diplomatic: Not causing bad feelings; having or showing an ability to deal with people politely.

32. Detailed: Caring about the details of a situation; being meticulous.

33. Cheerful: Feeling or showing happiness.

34. Consistent: Always acting or behaving in the same way.

35. Cultured: Having or showing good education, tastes, or manners.

36. Confident: Believing in one's own abilities.

37. Mediator: One that helps others come to agreement.

38. Musical: A musical artist, or someone who just enjoys music.

39. Mover: Someone that makes things happen.

40. Mixes easily: Someone who can socialize with other people of all types in a social setting.

41. Thoughtful: Mindful of the thoughts and feelings of others; considerate.

42. Tenacious: Very determined to do something; not easily stopped.

43. Talker: Someone who talks a lot.

44. Tolerant: Willing to accept feelings, habits, or beliefs that are different from your own.

45. Listener: Someone who is willing to listen to others.

46. Loyal: Having or showing complete and constant support for someone or something.

47. Leader: Someone that takes charge easily.

48. Lively: Active and energetic.

49. Contented: Happy and satisfied with what they have; not always striving for more.

50. Chief: A leader; someone who is often in charge.

51. Chart maker: Someone who loves charts, graphs, and lists.

52. Cute: Someone with a pleasing and youthful personality.

53. Perfectionist: Someone who wants everything to be done a certain way.

54. Pleasant: Friendly, likeable, easy-going.

55. Productive: Someone who gets a lot done.

56. Popular: Someone who is liked by many people.

Weaknesses

1. Undisciplined: A person who lacks order in the majority of their life.

2. Unsympathetic: Does not relate well, or care much, for the problems of others.

3. Unenthusiastic: Doesn't get excited about much.

4. Unforgiving: Holds a grudge; doesn't easily forget the faults of others.

5. Fussy: Must have minor details just right.

6. Fearful: May have many fears/anxieties.

7. Forgetful: Lack of memory that is usually tied to a lack of discipline, not bothering to mentally record things they don't consider fun.

8. Frank: Outspoken, straight-forward, blunt.

9. Impatient: Finds it hard to wait patiently for other people or events.

10. Insecure: Someone who lacks confidence.

11. Indecisive: Finds it hard to make a decision; needs a lot of input from others.

12. Interrupts: More of a talker than a listener; interrupts because they already know what you are going to say before you finish.

13. Plain: Someone without a lot of highs and lows; middle-of-the-road personality; doesn't show much emotion.
14. Pessimistic: Sees the downside of things, although they may still hope for the best.
15. Proud: High self-esteem; views him/herself as right most/all of the time.
16. Permissive: Lets people do what they want because of fear of being disliked.

17. Naïve: Child-like perspective; innocent; not a very deep person.
18. Negative attitude: Seeing only the downside of a situation; has a hard time seeing the positive side.
19. Nervy: Could be seen as obnoxious; someone with high confidence, lots of guts, but in a negative way.
20. Nonchalant: Easy-going; indifferent.

21. Worrier: Uncertain, troubled, anxious.
22. Withdrawn: People who tend to isolate themselves and need a lot of alone time.
23. Workaholic: Driven by accomplishment and reward; works too much or spends too much time pursuing other productive endeavors.
24. Wants credit: Thrives on the approval of others; an entertainer.

25. Too sensitive: Gets hurt easily; easily offended by others' comments or actions, even if well-meaning.
26. Tactless: Says offensive and/or inconsiderate things without caring how the other person feels.
27. Timid: Shy.
28. Talkative: Compulsive talker.

29. Doubtful: Uncertainty; lack of confidence.
30. Disorganized: Not a neat and orderly person.
31. Domineering: Takes control of people and/or situations; tells people what to do, even if they are not in charge.
32. Depressed: Someone who feels down most of the time, or who has times of deep, negative feelings.

33. Inconsistent: Not easy to predict what they will do; erratic; actions are often not based on logic.
34. Introvert: Thoughts and actions are focused inward; doesn't want to be the center of attention.
35. Intolerant: Doesn't accept the thoughts and opinions of other people; believes their way is the only way.
36. Indifferent: Doesn't care one way or the other about a decision that must be made.

37. Slow: Doesn't act or think quickly.

38. Stubborn: Not easily changed; holds to their opinion often, even in the face of other truth.

39. Show-off: Needs to be the center of attention; wants everyone to notice them.

40. Skeptical: Questions the motives behind something that is said or done.

41. Loner: Avoids people; would rather be alone.

42. Lord over others: Doesn't hesitate to let people know of something they are proud of, or of their authority over you.

43. Lazy: Doesn't have a lot of energy.

44. Loud: Not a quiet person.

45. Sluggish: Low energy; not much motivation.

46. Suspicious: Skeptical of people/situations; doesn't trust easily.

47. Short-tempered: Has a short fuse; angered easily.

48. Scatterbrained: Forgetful; flighty; doesn't concentrate and is not attentive.

49. **Revengeful (Vengeful):** Holds a grudge and wants to punish the offender, even if they do not follow through; withholds friendship and affection because of previous wrongs.

50. **Restless:** Excess energy; needs a new challenge all the time.

51. **Reluctant:** Hesitant to get involved.

52. **Rash:** Acts without thinking.

53. **Compromising:** Would rather go along with someone else's opinion, even if they feel they are right, just to avoid conflict.

54. **Critical:** Constantly judging or putting down others.

55. **Crafty:** Someone who can get what they want, one way or another.

56. **Changeable:** Short attention span; needs a lot of change in their life so they are not bored.

Appendix II
Descriptive Terms by Temperament Type

Choleric:

Strong-willed

Extrovert

Hot-tempered

Quick-thinking

Self-confident

Self-sufficient

Independent

Decisive

Opinionated

Visionary

Energetic

Purposeful

Results-oriented

Crusader

Direct

Firm

Authoritative

Uncaring

Uncompassionate

Choleric (continued):

Adventurous

Bossy

Persuasive

Competitive

Impatient

Outspoken

Proud

Forceful

Confidant

Argumentative

Mover and shaker

Workaholic

Tactless

Leader

Productive

Domineering

Tolerant

Commanding

Bold

Critical

Demanding

Sanguine:

Extrovert

Fun-loving

Energetic

Impulsive

Entertaining

Persuasive

Optimistic

Receptive

Relational

Animated

Excited

Accepting

Happy

Joyful

Talker

People-oriented

Late

Easily bored

Up and down

Friendly

Distracted

Unfocused

Sanguine (continued):

Competitive

Disorganized

Undisciplined

Emotional

Fashionable

Playful

Sociable

Forgetful

Refreshing

Interrupts

Promoter

Unpredictable

Spontaneous

Funny

Naïve

Cheerful

Wants credit

Inspiring

Moody

Scatterbrained

Popular

Melancholy:

Introverted

Logical

Analytical

Factual

Private

Withdrawn

Slow

Cautious

Reserved

Suspicious

Timid

Serious

Sensitive

Self-sacrificing

Gifted

Perfectionist

Organized

Fearful

Negative

Creative

Resourceful

Depressed

Melancholy (continued):

Controlled

Reserved

Unforgiving

Pessimistic

Planner

Scheduled

Loner

Disciplined

Detailed

Consistent

Deep

Chart maker

Moody

Focused

Conscientious

Careful

High standards

Intense

Resourceful

Consistent

Conservative

Judgmental

Phlegmatic:

Introvert

Calm

Unemotional

Easy-going

Friendly

Loyal

Peaceful

Slow

Accommodating

Procrastinator

Easy

Quiet

Routine

Uninvolved

Not driven

Sincere

Resists change

Predictable

Holds grudges

Stubborn

Practical

Concrete

Phlegmatic (continued):

Traditional

Stoic

Patient

Consistent

Adaptable

Indecisive

Submissive

Plain

Shy

Indifferent

Faithful

Reliable

Timid

Steadfast

Devoted

Dry sense of humor

Diplomatic

Mediator

Inoffensive

Lazy

Tolerant

Reluctant

Tom is available for seminars, workshops, training, consulting – whatever you or your company need to help you or your staff become better at relating well with other people. He can be reached at BugManTom@gmail.com, or by calling 281-804-9531.

www.ingramcontent.com/pod-product-compliance
Lightning Source LLC
Chambersburg PA
CBHW051548170526
45165CB00002B/932